PARABLE PRAISE PARTY

LOST and FOUND

written by Mary Rice Hopkins

illustrated by Dennas Davis

Faith Parenting Guide

Ages 4-7

Love

FaithKidz®

A Faith Parenting Guide can be found on page 34.

Faith Kidz® is an imprint of Cook Communications Ministries
Colorado Springs, Colorado 80918
Cook Communications, Paris, Ontario
Kingsway Communications, Eastbourne, England

First printing, 2004
Printed in Korea
2 3 4 5 6 7 8 9 10 Printing/Year 08 07 06 05 04

ISBN: 0781439906

Editor: Heather Gemmen
Interior Designer: Granite Design

There was a little lady who worked for every cent just to pay her grocery bill, just to pay her rent.

She asked her neighbors and her friends,
"Where is it? Do you know?"

8

No one told her where it was,
so she looked in every nook.

11

She dusted and she tidied up the dishes and the books.

13

She looked down in the basement,

in the chest, and up the stairs.

18

She looked in corners of the room—
yes, she looked everywhere!

Finally, the woman sat down on her favorite chair. She bowed her head and closed her eyes and said a little prayer.

She paused for just a moment,
then, fervent, she kept on:
She swept and cleaned and snooped around
till sunlight came at dawn.

24

And then she saw her little coin
shining, oh, so bright.
She jumped and laughed and carried on
as it sparkled in the light.

She called her friends to celebrate.
"Everyone! Please come!
It was lost and now it's found.
Come see what God has done!"

Jesus said,

"Suppose a woman has ten silver coins and loses one. Does she not light a lamp, sweep the house and search carefully until she finds it? And when she finds it, she calls her friends and neighbors together and says, 'Rejoice with me; I have found my lost coin.'

In the same way, I tell you, there is more rejoicing in the presence of the angels of God over one sinner who repents."

Luke 15:8–10

Oh Honey

Words & Music by
Mary Rice Hopkins

1. Up in the at - tic in ev - 'ry room Down in the base - ment with my broom I've
2. Oh my__ dear_ look at this mess I've looked eve - ry - where from East to West Un-
3. In ev - 'ry cran - ny place and nook E - ven in Gran - ny's fav - 'rite book

searched ev'ry - where from night till noon
til____ I find it I won't rest Oh where did my lit - tle bit - ty coin   go
With my__ dust mop I will look

30

31

Oh, Honey

Up in the attic in every room
Down in the basement with my broom
I've searched everywhere from night till noon
Oh where did my little bitty coin go
Where did my little bitty coin go

First Chorus
Oh honey I can't find my money
I'm sweeping and cleaning and feeling
  kind of blue
Oh honey I can't find my money
But when I find it I'm gonna kiss you
The angels will rejoice too

Oh my dear look at this mess
I've looked everywhere from East to West
Until I find it I won't rest
Oh where did my little bitty coin go
Oh where did my little bitty coin go

In every cranny place and nook
Even in granny's favorite book
With my dust mop I will look
Where did my little bitty coin go
Where did my little bitty coin go

Jump for joy it's been found
With every girl and boy in town
When one is lost and turns around
Rejoice with them in heaven
Rejoice with them in heaven

Second Chorus
Oh honey now I've found my money
Now I'm not feeling so blue
Oh honey I've found my money
Now I've found it I'm gonna kiss you
The angels are rejoicing too
Rejoicing too rejoicing too rejoicing too

33

LOST AND FOUND

Ages: 4-7

Life Issue: I want my children to know that God's love
will always seek them out.

Spiritual Building Block: Love

Do the following sight activities to help your children understand God's care for them:

Sight: After you finish reading this book to your children, go through the story again. This time, invite your kids to search for certain items on each page. (For example, have them look for a wagon on page 9 and a key on page 13.) Some items will be harder to find than others, but encourage your kids to keep looking until they find each item (keeping in mind the attention span appropriate for their age group).

Tell your kids that God loves all people so much that he will never, ever give up searching for any lost person. And that includes each of your children. God keeps seeking his loved ones, and when he finds them, he gives them a big hug (as you do to your child) and celebrates that they have come home.

Hide coins in your children's rooms. Time them to see how long it takes to find the coins. When they are close say hot, and when they are not close say cold. After they find what is hidden, celebrate together by having a party—even if it's just a party for two. Make sure your kids understand that being found by God causes all of heaven to celebrate.

Sound: Enjoy the first song on the CD together. Then start the song over and play this game: Sing one line and have your children sing the next line. Continue until the song is completed.

Besides having fun together and reinforcing the message of this parable as you do this exercise, you will be using music and rhythm to increase your children's development for both reading skills and mathematical aptitude.

At the end of your time of singing, do not forget to celebrate together the joy and love that comes from seeing something lost being found!

Touch: After you enjoy the story together, turn to page 28. Get a blank piece of paper and ask your children to help you copy the verse. You write most of the words, but ask your children to fill in the words that are appropriate to their reading level.

After the verse is written, ask your children to help you read the verse out loud. You read the words that you wrote and let your children read the words that they wrote. Ask your children to tell you what the passage is about. You want to help them in their comprehension of the verse not only to increase their reading ability, but to convey the biblical message of God's love for them.

You can adapt this activity by covering certain words in the book with a piece of paper. Have your children guess what the covered word is.